HUMAN TRAFFICKING 101

HUMAN TRAFFICKING 101

Stories, Stats, and Solutions

AMY JOY

Amy Joy

CONTENTS

Acknowledgements 1

Prolog 3

Introduction 9

1 What is Human Trafficking? 11

2 The Scope 22

3 The United States 25

4 Sex Trafficking 29

5 Labor Trafficking 33

6 In Plain Site 40

7 Demand 44

8 Social Media 49

9 Predators/Traffickers 55

10 Warning Signs 62

11 How to Report 70

12 Common Threads 72

13 Adverse Childhood Experiences Study (ACE's) 84

14 Healing & Intervention Techniques 89

Epilog 96

Terminology 97

Assessment Questions 103

References 107

Acknowledgements

There is not enough space on these pages to thank all the people who have had a wonderful impact on my life. I cannot print this book without recognizing my sweet, kind, graceful, fabulous friends Charlotte and Michele. From one decade to the next, the two of you have been bright lights in my often, dark world. Thank you for just being the wonderful women God created you to be and hanging with this nutty girl. I love you both!!

To my adventurous, groovy, edgy, smart, sweet, loving children, you will always be my sweet baby girl and boy!! You made the fight worth it! You will always have my heart!

To my amazing therapist and confidant Virginia, thank you! Thank you for creating a safe, loving place for me to heal and grow. Thank you for giving me the strength to be vulnerable and the tools to be strong. You are one of the strongest, sweetest, authentic women I have ever known. You are a breath of fresh air and a place of rest. You are my rock!

And of course, I could not make it through this world

without the guiding love of my sweet grandmother, Opal. You are beyond all that I could possibly have wanted in a mother. You let me experience what it was to be a daughter. Thank you for loving me like Jesus loves! You have saved my life in more ways than one. I love you!

Prolog

I want to thank you for taking the time to become educated on this very important social issue. If you are like me when I first heard of human trafficking, you may think this issue is reserved for foreigners and third-world nations. It wasn't until I attended a women's retreat and heard a missionary speaking about what human trafficking truly is here in the United States, that I realized how close to home this really was and is.

My Story

In 2011, I attended a women's retreat with the intention of slipping away for a weekend of relaxation and fellowship with my girlfriends. I had no idea when I signed up for this retreat that human trafficking was on the agenda. Eight friends from church and I made our way up to the frozen tundra of Northern Michigan to gain some insight and trade coupons. You see, women's retreats are just camps for big girls. Instead of Elmer's glue and macaroni necklaces, we had classes in couponing and Divorce Care. It was a big surprise when we arrived at the retreat center and I realized the entire weekend was themed around human trafficking. The main speaker for the weekend was a missionary in the field of helping victims of human trafficking. I had just gone through a very long and difficult divorce and decided to attend the Divorce Care class, even though I had been through the course five times already. The sixth time is a charm! I arrived at the class and put my things down, but something was nagging at me, calling me to go listen to the missionary who was speaking in the main auditorium. I picked up my things and walked back to hear the missionary. There was only one person from my group in that room and she was...is, my dearest friend. I sat down and began to listen to the missionary talk about human trafficking, but felt that she was talking about *me*, my life and my experience. I KNEW this, all of this, I just had no idea it had been defined and that it was a law. It was all so raw and devastating and liberating! My spirit spilled out and broke wide open that weekend. I remember crying and slobbering all over my dear friend. I knew from those first raw moments that my past; my disgusting, shameful, dirty past was not meant to just sit and be ugly. It had to mean something, anything.

Already enrolled in a program for social work at a university, I found myself even more engrossed in the cultural and familial dynamics of human trafficking. I spent the next several months in deep, deep research. I continue to research daily, but those first few months were intense. With some cool connections from the retreat and the advice of my friend, I went back to that retreat center the following year and gave my first presentation on human trafficking.

You may be asking yourself, "Why on earth did the missionary's words have such an impact?" Well, since you asked, I'll tell you. When I was almost fourteen years old, my father was arrested and sent to jail for raping my friend. From the moment he was arrested until the moment I had heard the missionary tell of the horrors of human trafficking, I had not uttered a word about what had happened to me. In fact, I had, with great difficulty, recanted, retracted, and denied any part of being abused. For more than twenty years I said nothing and felt a great deal of sorrow and shame for what *I* had done.

You see, I told. Me, the one who was supposed to keep all the secrets. "Family business is family business!", he constantly barked at us. Never knowing what he was planning next, I tried to be "on guard", forever looking out for a hair-pulling, a smack on the back of the head, or a squeeze so hard it brought us to our knees. I often found myself staring out the kitchen window, not paying attention like I should, and then, like a bolt of lightning, he would grab me. There is more, but that is all you need for now.

I never told. Not until my friend came over, that is. I grew up believing that what was happening was the norm. I thought everybody had a dad like mine. They were all kind of mean and sneaky and sometimes needed things we didn't understand. He was kind sometimes too, though, and I would spend my days hoping he was going to be nice that day. At times, he played with me in the yard throwing a baseball back and forth. He taught me how to build furniture, not great furniture, but good enough for a ten-year old. He taught me math and real estate and how to calculate interest rates. There were good things, but thinking back on it now, there weren't enough to erase the bad things.

The bad things over took my adolescence. I spent my middle school years calculating how much Vodka could help me pass out for the night and still let me function in school the next day. I spent a lot time finding people and things to fill the gaps of love and support; the missing pieces of my every day. My mother had passed away when I was around two-years old and since that time, my father bounced from one single mother to another. By the time middle school rolled around, the last step-mother and siblings had all moved out. It was just me....and him.

When that missionary began talking I understood it because over the years I had become my father's bait; his recruiter. It was a constant badgering to bring friends over. He would get us drunk and then, well, you can figure out the rest. The thing was, none of my friends ever told, they just never came back. Over Christmas break, when I was thirteen, that all changed. The last friend I brought over changed everything. He did his usual get us drunk routine. I tried desperately to drag her off the couch and into my room for the night, but he kept pulling her back to his lap and with a final yell, I knew I couldn't do anything to help her. Retreating to my room was the only option left. I then watched, from the crack in my door, as he carried my friend's limp body to his room and got into bed with her.

Whenever I brought a friend over for him, I would get rewarded. The next morning, my reward was we got to go bowling. We were dropped off at the bowling alley, and then she told me everything. I already knew but pretended like I didn't. She made me promise not to tell but I did not keep that promise.

The following Monday I went into the counseling office at school and asked the counselor, "Hypothetically speaking, what would happen if...?" and I laid out the scenario from the weekend before. It was my chance. I only had one shot at making it out without it being me it had happened to. It wasn't me, it was her; *her* story was the only thing that could save me.

The following two weeks, nothing happened, or so I thought. There were detectives outside of our home watching everything that was happening. My father worked afternoons and shortly after I got home from school, he left for work and would return around midnight. But this is where the system fell apart for me. Instead of someone coming to my home to make sure I was okay, I received a phone call from Child Protective Services. The man on the other end asked me if I knew my father had been arrested that afternoon, and I quickly told him "No." The man then asked me to give him the name and number of someone they could call to come and pick me up. It took a few minutes, but I was able to come up with friends of the family who we hadn't seen in quite a while. The only family I was close to was my grandparents on my mother's side, but there was no way I wanted them to know that any of this was happening to me. This was such a shameful part of me.

It didn't take long after hanging up with the CPS worker to realize that my life was forever changed. It did not come with the hope of a happy ending, but with more dread and awful foreboding, more than anything I had ever experienced. The following day, my father, now bailed out of jail, was sitting next to me on a couch. He told me "You have ruined my f***ing life", repeatedly. I totally believed him and spent the next several years trying to make it up to him and the next twenty years completely silent about the horrors I endured through childhood.

It wasn't until that retreat that God broke open the heart of a little girl, wounded and crying for three decades, to release what is now the greatest reward I could have ever imagined. I now help girls, boys, men, and women just like me. I get to educate professionals and community members on how to help victims of trafficking and abuse. Every time I speak and tell my story, a little piece of that little girl's heart is mended.

There is hope for girls like me. There is life in speaking truth over the lost and the broken. I am here today because God really can turn burnt, disgusting horror into a beautiful, living testimony. I hope you find a little of that hope and beauty as you read this book.

Introduction

Human trafficking has always been a part of human history. The first recorded incident of human trafficking was in the Bible when Joseph was sold into slavery by his brothers. While it has always been an evil and vile activity, it has become a whole new, bigger, more heinous beast than anyone could have fathomed. The increase in access to pornography, ability for predators to access vulnerable people from across the globe, and lack of accountability for buyers and suppliers of the human trafficking are just a few of the major issues that have created one of the world's largest criminal industries. In the past 5 years reports of suspected child sex trafficking has risen 846% and directly correlated to increased use of internet to sell children for sex (National Center for Missing and Exploited Children, 2018) . The National Center for Missing and Exploited Children reported more than 2.3 million reports of suspected child sexual exploitation to law enforcement and analyzed more than 108 million images and videos depicting apparent child pornography (Gerassi, 2015). Human trafficking is complicated and every case is unique, making this horrific crime difficult to detect and fix. However, knowing the signs, understanding the basic dynamics of trafficking, and knowing how to respond are the keys to making a dent in this evil practice and protecting YOUR loved ones.

By reading this book, you will learn how human trafficking is defined by the United States Federal Government, how these laws may differ from your State laws and how to identify and respond when you suspect there is a case of human trafficking in your community. There are examples and tips along the way to help you find quick references for practice.

CHAPTER 1

What is Human Trafficking?

Human trafficking exists in every corner of the world, but looks very different depending on the geographic region, economy, and other socio-economic situations. In many underdeveloped countries like portions of Africa, Asia, and South America; labor trafficking occurs most frequently. Labor trafficking is the act of exploiting others for manual or physical work. Those who are exploited get paid little or nothing at all and many are given only the basic needs required to survive. Sex trafficking occurs mostly in countries with well-developed economic systems. Examples include the United States, Canada, parts of Europe, and Australia.

The first United States Federal law on human trafficking was adopted in the year 2000 with the passage of the Trafficking Victim's Protection Act (TVPA, 2000). This federal law stated that **one element from each of the three categories: An act of, By means of and For the purpose of** has to be present in order for the federal government to classify a crime as human trafficking.

What is Human Trafficking?

Act of...	Means of...	Purpose of...
• Recruiting	• Force	• Exploitation
• Harboring	• Fraud	• Involuntary servitude
• Transporting	• Coercion	
• Providing		• Forced military
• Obtaining		• Debt bondage
• Selling		

There must be an **act** of recruiting, harboring, transporting, providing, obtaining, or selling; by the **means** of force, fraud, or coercion; for the **purpose** of sexual or labor exploitation, involuntary servitude, forced military service, or debt bondage.

Again, only one element from each category has to be present for it to be classified as a human trafficking crime.

Purpose of...

Exploitation: All human trafficking has an element of exploitation. This simply means that someone is gaining (usually money) from someone else's loss (loss of freedom).

Involuntary Servitude: In close relation to debt bondage, this often refers to a victim of trafficking having to work either to pay off a debt or under some form of coercion, where the trafficker gains financially and the victim is not free to leave.

Forced Military Service: We do not see this here in the United States, but it is often utilized in parts of the world where there are loosely formed military groups, smaller tribes at war, and areas where military officials are engaged in criminal activity.

Debt bondage is often associated with those seeking a job opportunity or better employment. They are sold a promise of a better wages, travel, or upward mobility and delivered a life of slavery and deprivation.

Example

Emily lives in Germany and finds an advertisement in the paper. It is for a job opportunity in the United States. The ad reads "Make great money in the United States as a waitress." Emily calls who she thinks is a job recruiter, but is truly a trafficker, and requests more information. She attends a meeting that appears very professional. Emily feels this is a great opportunity and arranges to pay the job recruiter $1,000.00 for transportation costs and providing legal documentation to enter the United States. Being assured that everything is good to go, Emily travels to the United States believing she will be working as a waitress and making enough money to send home to help her family. When she arrives, however, her documents are taken from her and she is told she must work in a strip club. She is told that her safe passage to the United States cost her job recruiter, a.k.a. trafficker, more than $2,000.00 and she must pay the balance before she is free to leave. This is *Debt Bondage* and the debt rarely ever diminishes or goes away. Emily is told that if she runs or tries to get help, the police will deport her or send her to prison. She is also threatened with physical violence to herself and her family. Because the trafficker has ties to Emily's home country, she knows he can harm her family. Threats, beatings, and rape is now "the life" of Emily.

Side note:

In debt bondage, the debt never goes away. The victim of trafficking/debt bondage is trapped because the trafficker begins to charge the victim for shelter, food, clothing and anything else provided by the trafficker.

Side note:

Many who enter foreign nations, for the purposes of being trafficked, do so with legal documents; passports, T-Visa, Student Visa, etc.

By Means of...

Force – this is exactly what it seems. It means that someone has been or is being physically taken and/or held against their will as well as beaten, raped, and/or tortured to keep them from being free.

Fraud – often associated with debt bondage, this is basically tricking someone. A trafficker promised one thing (a job, a house, a lifestyle, or simply a safe place to sleep) and delivered something completely different, often a life of servitude, rape, and torture.

Coercion – often referred to as the process of "boy-friending" or "grooming" into "the life" or "the game." Coercion and fraud are most often the pieces associated with human trafficking here in the United States.

Force is most often associated with trafficking through media and news outlets but really, only about 3% of those trafficked here in the United States are kidnapped (Troopers, January 21, 2018). Rape, beatings, torture, and restraint are often used after a victim has been coerced or tricked into trafficking. About 62% are coerced or tricked (fraud), and approximately 35% of those trafficked are done so by their own family members.

The Act of...

The *Act* of...refers to any activity associated with initiating, participating, facilitating, or maintaining an operation for the purposes of exploitation. Any person found to be conducting any of these activities in conjunction with the *purpose* of...can be convicted of a human trafficking crime. Those activities include recruiting, harboring, transporting, providing, obtaining, or selling of individuals. For example, if "Trafficker Joe" (yes, fictitious name) calls up his mother and asks her to watch two sixteen-year old girls (victims of sex trafficking) because he needs to run some errands, Trafficker Joe's Mother is now part of the human trafficking chain and can be charged with harboring two victims of sex trafficking.

The federal government says you must have at least one element from each section for it to be classified as a human trafficking crime. The three sections are the *act* of, the *means* of, and the *purpose* of...or ... **any commercial sex act with a person under the age of 18**. If there is a child being exploited through pornography, a strip club, sold online for sex, or any other commercial sex act, they are automatically considered victims of human trafficking and entitled to all the same services and protections as any other victim, and they do NOT have to prove by which *means* (force, fraud, or coercion) they were trafficked (Dr. Dominique Roe-Sepowitz, et al., 2017).

Commercial sex: exchange of any sex acts for an item of value.

Item of Value: includes, but is not limited to money, drugs, transportation, food, or shelter.

Side note:

At the present time, there are 27 States who can, and often do, pick up and prosecute girls and boys for prostitution. Many fifteen, sixteen, and seventeen-year-olds have been picked up and prosecuted, rather than protected.

You have probably heard the term "modern-day slavery". If you are like me before I learned what this really was, you may be visualizing slavery where people are bought and sold like chattel. In some parts of the globe this is still prevalent, but here in the United States and other well-industrialized nations, it simply means "one who is physically, emotionally, or

psychologically unable to free one's self from their captor/
trafficker" (Gerassi, 2015).

Human trafficking is not limited by race, color or creed.
It does not care how old or young you are, whether you are
rich or poor, or from what neighborhood you come. Human
trafficking happens everywhere and can happen to anyone. It
crosses all socio-economic statuses, races, cultures, and bor-
ders. There are some known indicators that create greater vulnerabilities in people, but we will discuss this a little later.
"The only way not to find human trafficking in your community, is simply not to look for it" (documentary, Playground,
2007).

Several years ago, as we began teaching community leaders
and members, more and more people were becoming aware
of the dynamics involved with human trafficking, but there
was some confusion between what human trafficking was and
how it differed from other crimes. We decided to break it
down for you. Human trafficking activities often include
other crimes and associated activities, but are not exclusively
these things; transportation, sexual abuse, low wages, or void
of a trafficker.

Let me explain. If I were to pay someone $3,000.00 to pro-
vide passage from Mexico into the United States without legal
documents and I arrive safely and am free to go, it is *smuggling*
not human trafficking. However, if I get to the United States
and the person I paid now says I owe them additional money

and must work to pay it off before I am free to leave, it is debt bondage and we now have human trafficking.

Transportation is often a part of the process of sex trafficking. Sex traffickers in the United States move their victims to up to 17 states, with an average of 2.76 states, for the purposes of prostituting victims (Dr. Dominique Roe-Sepowitz, et al., 2017). Many travel patterns, or what are called *circuits*, often stay within certain trafficking boundaries, depending on gang activity and territorial claims. For instance, there is a *circuit* that runs through the East Coast; West Coast, Southern states; and Northern states. One-third of sex trafficking victims, who were part of the Six-Year Analysis of Sex Traffickers of Minors (2017), were transported across state lines.

It is not familial sex abuse, although it often starts here (Dr. Dominique Roe-Sepowitz, et al., 2017) (Child Welfare and Human Trafficking; Issue Brief, 2015). Sexual abuse in the home conditions children from an early age to accept the lies, coercion, false promises, and other psychologically damaging behaviors brought to them by traffickers. Those who are sexually abused as children present greater vulnerabilities than those who have not been abused. Their developing brains are often impacted by repeated trauma and have a diminished capacity, or are unable to process new information, discern danger from safety, control emotion and impulse, and access help.

Human trafficking can include, but is not exclusively, adult labor for low pay (Bender, 2018) (Project, 2016). A great example of this is one day a couple of years ago, a young lady said to me "this lady told me I could come and clean her apartment and she would give me 150 dollars. I got there and cleaned her apartment so good, but she only gave me 50 bucks." I looked at the young lady for a moment and asked, "were you able to leave?" She said "yes." "Did you have to go back?" I asked. She said "no." I told her I was sorry she had been taken advantage of, but that was not human trafficking. It really stinks to be used this way, but the fact is, this young lady was free to come and go as she saw fit and did not have to work for little or no pay. It was her choice. Was she taken advantage of? Sure, but it was not human trafficking.

Human trafficking is not human trafficking without a *trafficker* (a controller, captor, etc.). If, for example, Kasie, a 21-year-old woman is working as a sex worker, posting her advertisements online, making her own "dates," in control of her own money, and in every way has complete agency over her own life, she is engaging in prostitution. Prostitution is a crime in most areas of the United States. Those who choose prostitution, work right alongside those who are trafficked. Some do choose "the life" or "the game." Chances are though, Kasie did not start out on her own or at the age of twenty-one, but most likely with a trafficker/pimp and at a much younger age.

Take-aways

- Human trafficking is global, national, and local. It looks differently depending on the geographic region and economy.
- The United States Federal government created the Trafficking Victim's Protection Act in 2000. One element from each category (Act of, by Means of, and Purpose of) must be present for a crime to be classified as a human trafficking crime; or anyone under the age of 18 who is participating in a commercial sex act.
- Smuggling, familial sexual abuse, and prostitution are crimes often associated with human trafficking, but are not these things exclusively.

CHAPTER 2

The Scope

The Scope

Depending upon the resource used, the numbers related to human trafficking can vary widely. It is a very underreported, underground crime. Most traffickers, okay no traffickers, are like "hey, I've got six girls." They do not self-disclose. Traffickers are often charged and prosecuted for crimes associated with trafficking but not necessarily for the actual crime of human trafficking. Drug, weapon, and assault related charges are easier to prosecute and convict than those of exploitation. Several challenges present themselves when a human trafficking case is brought to court. One, many victims of trafficking, particularly sex trafficking, are psychologically attached to their trafficker and can refuse to testify. If a victim does decide to testify, they often have difficulty telling their story, resulting in them appearing unbelievable or not credible to a judge or jury. When trauma occurs, over time the emotional center of the brain, where memories are downloaded and processed, begins to deteriorate. The language center of the brain may shut down and memories, if they can be verbalized, come out distorted and in illogical order (Bessel Van Der Kolk, 2014).

- There are approximately 21-45 million people enslaved in the world today and about every 30 seconds someone new is forced, tricked or coerced into human trafficking(State, 2016).
- There are approximately one million new victims of human trafficking every year.
- There are more than 750,000 child predators on the internet at any given moment('Grooming' is a Gateway to Online Child Sex Trafficking, 2018).
- Human trafficking is the fastest growing criminal industry in the world, second only to guns and drug trafficking(Project, 2016). The data shows that human trafficking and drugs often go hand in hand.
- Human trafficking generates upwards of $150 billion dollars per year(State, 2016). Traffickers have an incredible amount of resources at their disposal. A sex trafficker in the United States can make as much as $300,000 from one victim.

Take-aways:

- Human trafficking is a very underreported crime and data can vary widely
- Traffickers are plentiful and have a great deal of monetary resources

CHAPTER 3

The United States

While human trafficking takes on several different forms, there are two major forms of trafficking here in the United States: *Sex trafficking* and *labor trafficking* (Project, 2016). Sex trafficking is any activity (recruiting, harboring, transporting, providing, obtaining, or selling), by means of force, fraud, or coercion, for the purposes of exploiting people in the commercial sex industry. The term *commercial* here means the exchanging of sexual acts for tangible goods (money, material supply, food, shelter, etc.). Labor trafficking is any activity (recruiting, harboring, transporting, providing, obtaining, or selling), by means of force, fraud, or coercion, for the purposes of the buying and selling of individuals for the purposes of involuntary servitude, debt bondage, or forced military. Sex trafficking is the most common form of trafficking here in the United States, as well as in other well-industrialized nations (European nations, Canada, Australia, etc.) (Gerassi, 2015).

The United States is the number one destination for Americans seeking sex with children (International,

2018) (Project, 2016). 15-20 years ago, most predators from the United States would have to travel outside of the country to do the kinds of sex acts to children they can easily do now in the community where they live. Having sex with children, here in the U.S., is as easy as ordering a pizza. The United States is one of the world's largest destinations for sex tourism. *Sex tourism* simply means that someone has left their home country or state for the specific purpose of having sex with a child, or paying for sex with an adult, where it is expressly prohibited. So, not only do Americans no longer have to travel outside of the country, but people from other countries are coming here to have sex with American children.

- Human trafficking has been reported in all 50 states. No city, county, or state is immune to human trafficking(Project, 2016). Even in very rural parts of the country, children are bought and sold for sexual and laborious purposes.
- Every year within the United States, according to the national reporting agency, The Polaris Project, approximately 300,000 children are traded for sex.
- The average daily quota (the amount of money required by a victim to receive in exchange for sexual acts) is around $600.
- Domestic victims of trafficking, those who were born here or who are lawful citizens of the United States, represent 77-90% of those who are trafficked(Dr. Dominique Roe-Sepowitz, et al., 2017).
- Currently, beds available for minor victims of sex trafficking within the United States are so rare, they would

only be able to serve less than one-percent of victims. To date, there are around 1,000 beds available located in anything from drop-in centers to long-term care facilities(International, 2018).

- About 80% of those trafficked in the United States are female and approximately half are children under the age of 18. A recent study showed that nearly 44% of those under the age of 18 who are trafficked are boys (St. John University Study, 2017).

Traffickers know how to bring out and identify vulnerabilities in people (Child Welfare and Human Trafficking; Issue Brief, 2015) (Foster Care & Human Trafficking, 2017). Runaway and "throwaway" children are big targets for traffickers because they are extremely vulnerable. Here in the United States, there are approximately 1.8 million children who are consistently missing (National Center for Missing and Exploited Children, 2018). One-third of these children are called "throwaway" children because nobody has reported them missing. In many states, if a child is over the age of fourteen, a parent or guardian does not have to report them missing. We find them when they either show up in crisis somewhere like a pregnancy center or an emergency department, or are found dead. Leading causes of early death are drug overdose, murder, suicide, untreated physical injury or treatable transmittable diseases.

The average age of a child who is forced, tricked, or coerced into sex trafficking is 11-13 years old. The trend in boys being sexually trafficking is steadily increasing and the point of entry age is younger than girls (St. John University Conference, 2017). The data shows that boys make up nearly 44% of those trafficked under the age of 18. The increased rate of infant, toddler, and child rape in the porn industry has been linked to the increased rate of boys and girls trafficked (Handrahan, 2017). Pornographic materials continue to be more and more violent, depict more scenarios of incest, and involve younger and younger children. The rate of demand for the rape and torture of children has led to an increased rate in the production and distribution of child pornography. It has also led to an increased rate in those seeking sex from children beyond the computer screen.

Take-aways

- The United States is a destination country for sex traffickers (suppliers) and sex tourists (buyers).
- There are approximately 1 million victims of trafficking in the United States.
- Sex trafficking is the most common form of trafficking in the United States.
- Domestic victims make up the majority of those trafficked.
- Runaway, throwaway, foster care, and sexually abused children are among the most vulnerable trafficking victims.

CHAPTER 4

Sex Trafficking

Sex trafficking is the most common form of trafficking here in the United States (Project, 2016). As a nation, we lead the world in pornography production and distribution; one of the leading causes for demand and the purchase of children for sex. Many assume those from other countries are most frequently trafficked for the purpose of sexual servitude, but that is far from reality. *Domestic* victims; our sons, daughters, nieces, nephews, grandchildren, etc. are bought and sold in the commercial sex industry a million times over, right here their own country.

Common forms of reported sex trafficking include:

- **Any Commercial Sex Act with a Child**
- **Pornography**
- **Massage Parlors**
- **Spas**
- **Escort Agencies**
- **Pimp-Controlled Prostitution**
- **Online Solicitation**

- **Residential Brothels**

Common locations used for the purpose of sex trafficking:

- **Hotel Rooms**
- **Outcall Locations**
- **Houses**
- **Streets**
- **Apartments**
- **Other**

Online Solicitation

Online solicitation is a major player when it comes to recruiting and selling victims. Due to the recent lawsuits and events surrounding Backpage.com, there has been a slight reduction in the number of children and adults being sold on so-called "community sites" or online platforms. (For more information about Backpage.com, please look up the documentary, "I am Jane Doe".) However, this does not tell the whole story. Traffickers are digging deeper into the Dark Web to sell and trade people for sex; develop and distribute child pornography; and collaborate with other predators on how to best access children, instruct each other on what acts to do at what ages, and so on. The internet has magnified one's ability to connect with almost anyone in the world. Whether around the world or down the street, most predators have access to the same technology and services we use to run our businesses, teach our kids, and connect with friends and family. Predators/traffickers know how to use technology for their own gain; destroying the lives of loved ones in the process.

Residential Brothels

Residential brothels are easy for traffickers to start and maintain, particularly if those operating the brothel are family members.

Example

In the middle of a very cold Michigan winter, very early in the morning, Marie, a young girl just over 18 years old opened her front door and ran as fast as she could. Dressed in only her shorts, socks, and a tank top she saw an opportunity to escape; and did. She saw a light on at the house across the street and took a chance they might let her in. It was 5 A.M. and the sun was not up yet, so Marie tried to be as quiet as she could when she knocked on the door. Thankfully, the resident of the house opened the door and recognized that something was very wrong. The neighbor let her in and helped her reach out to a local shelter for help, but the shelter was full. The Director called Restoration Place, our nonprofit agency, and we were able to find a bed for her. It took some coordination to get her to a safe house, but we were able to arrange transportation, shelter, and clothing. When we arrived to get her out of the neighbor's home and to a safe house, she had just had enough. She could not take another night of the hell she had been living. Even though it had been several hours since the phone calls were first initiated, Marie was alert, nervous, scared and with adrenaline rushing through her, told us her story. Every night for six years, Marie was sold for sex by her very own mother and stepfather. Her mother used a cell phone to set up "dates" for Marie, and the johns would come to the house. She was trapped in that house and had a quota of $500 a night. Her parents used the money to support their drug addiction and often forced Marie to use cocaine. Only having been to school for three years and just barely a legal adult, she had slipped through the cracks of child protective services, the local school district, and every community she had lived. Nobody was aware that this young lady even existed until she found the courage to run. Unfortunately, this happens in every corner of America and is just one example of a residential brothel.

Take-aways

- Pornography is one of the leading avenues of demand for child sex trafficking.
- Social media plays a huge role in the initial contact, grooming process, and subsequent selling of children for sexual purposes.
- There are many different forms of sex trafficking present in the United States.
- Residential brothels may have as few as one victim.

CHAPTER 5

Labor Trafficking

Labor trafficking is most prevalent where traffickers can easily exploit areas that have experienced violence, war, natural disasters, lack of employment, lack of education, lack of opportunity, and poverty (Soper, 2018). As a nation, the United States is a primary buyer of the products produced and distributed by slaves, which include items like chocolate, coffee, shoes, clothing, etc.

Forms of reported Labor Trafficking include the following industries:

- **Restaurants/Bars**
- **Hotels**
- **Agriculture**
- **Construction**
- **Traveling Sales Crews**
- **Begging**
- **Armed Services**
- **Circus Performers**
- **Folk Dancers**

- **Choir Singers**

Circus performers, Folk dancers, and Choir singers, oh my!

I know you are probably thinking, "Seriously? Circus performers, folk dancers, and choir singers? I would love to sing forever!" Unfortunately, these are not the industries we often think they are. These groups often begin in third-world countries where traffickers go into very poor villages and identify talents in young children. Traffickers tell the parents that their children will get to travel the world, be educated, and send loads of money home for the family and community. Unsuspecting and desperate parents are often coerced into giving up their children and before they realize it, traffickers have stolen the community's next generation. These groups then travel the world performing for others, but they are generally not educated, do not receive money to send back to their families, and are trapped in a life of servitude.

Begging

Panhandlers, in many cities around the country, are groups of very well-organized trafficking rings. Traffickers will exploit the homeless and offer them shelter, food, and often drugs in exchange for spending every day, all day, on the street begging strangers for money (Gerassi, 2015). Many times, the same vehicles are seen dropping off and picking up the same people with the same signs, in the same locations, day after day. To connect with these folks, outreach teams can take items like underwear, socks, bottled water, and food. It is important to build trust when working with people who are being exploited as this is the best way to reach out and care for them. Building relationships also lets them know that, when they are ready, they have access to someone who can help.

Traveling Sales Crews

Transportation, while not always a part of human trafficking, is often used to evade authorities and keep victims unsteady. Victims are often transported from one city to another on a regular basis. This holds victims in a continued state of vulnerability and confusion. Traffickers of traveling sales crews will often threaten their victims with being left in the middle of the desert or other deserted areas.

Example

The summer I turned thirteen-years old, I desperately wanted a job, and in the 1980's, in the summer it was expected that I have a job. Most kids mowed lawns, delivered newspapers, or babysat... not me! The year before I had a job as a short-order cook in a Mexican restaurant. I loved it! At only twelve-years old, the owners reported that I was their niece and I could then work in the 'family' business for a certain number of hours per week. The following summer however, the restaurant was no longer in business. I did not like kids, so babysitting was out for me. I decided to look in the classifieds for a job. That's in the newspaper for any who may be unfamiliar with how to look for a job in any other place but the internet. I quickly found an ad that read "student help wanted for the summer" and called the number immediately.

Now the following example is full of red flags and if this was going on today, I am sure somebody would have put a stop to it. However, it was the 1980s and human trafficking hadn't even been defined yet, so the signs went unnoticed and unaddressed.

When I called the phone number, a woman answered and was very pleased I had called. They needed young people who were willing to work. Tammy, the woman who answered, told me she would pick me up in the morning. I thought this was fantastic! The next morning came and here is how the next two months went.

Tammy, along with a man in his 40s or 50s who appeared to be her boyfriend, and a younger man in his early twenties were the only adults with whom I ever had contact. Between the three of them, they drove two vans and a pickup truck and went around to mostly impoverished neighborhoods to pick up children, ages 8 through 15. I did not live in an impoverished area, but I had answered the ad. Every morning around 7:00 A.M. a van, usually with Tammy driving, would pick me up at the end of my driveway.

After rounding up about two dozen kids, we were driven to very affluent neighborhoods. The houses were gigantic and stunning. Dropped off at the end of these glimmering streets, we were instructed to sell Tootsie Roll Banks door to door for a dollar each. If you don't know what a Tootsie Roll Bank is, just visit your local supermarket and you can probably find one. They are just what they sound like, big Tootsie Rolls made of cardboard and turned into piggy banks, and of course had Tootsie Roll candies stuffed inside.

At each house we visited we were to tell people that all the money went to a safe house for women. We were given pieces of paper that indicated we were helping some nonprofit that I am sure did not exist. Occasionally, the van would come whizzing by and Tammy would yell, "get in!" Someone had called the cops!

Tammy was very sweet, but always crying. The older man she was with yelled at her a lot and always in some foreign language. To compound issues, Tammy did not know how to count. At the end of each day, another older girl and I were brought back to the hotel room where Tammy and her man were living. We were trusted to count the money. I remember thinking "this is crazy and a little scary", but I had a job, and that's what mattered to my thirteen-year-old brain. One day the crew stopped picking us up. My guess is that the cops got wind of what they were doing and they were chased out of town. I don't know for sure what happened to Tammy and the two men, but I sure am grateful it ended the way it did. This story has many red flags, but traveling sales crews are no longer as obvious as an eight-year old showing up on your doorstep selling items for a fake agency.

Today, traveling sales crews are made up primarily of 17-24

year-olds who are sold on a lifestyle. Youth who are homeless, runaways, and those disconnected from family support are often targeted. They are told they will travel the country, live in hotel rooms, and make a lot of money. Drugs, alcohol, and sexual exploitation are often part of this lifestyle. These young adults may show up on your doorstep selling household cleaning supplies, beauty products, magazines, etc. They will tell you an elaborate story about earning points for a scholarship or internship. They may ask you to use the bathroom or for something to drink, which are huge red flags. Get them talking. Ask about their program, where they have come from, their dreams for the future, etc. Ask if they are safe or need help. Once they have left, call your local township and ask if there are any groups licensed to sell in your neighborhood and call the police if you suspect it is not legitimate. You should also contact the Human Trafficking Hotline (1-888-3737-888), but we will go over this in more detail later.

Restaurants, bars, nail salons, spas, and massage parlors.

A good tip for finding out if individuals are being exploited in one of these industries is to find the bathroom farthest from the front. Look for evidence of people living on the premises. Items like toothbrushes, shampoo, and bedding are a good indication that those who work there, also live there. By all means, do not go rifling through their trash. Be diligent, be respectful, and report to the Human Trafficking Hotline (1-888-3737-888) if anything seems out of the ordinary. Also, look for signage that is of very low quality, such as outdoor signs made of plywood and spray paint. I have even seen a massage parlor write their outdoor advertisement on poster board with a sharpie. Most of the Asian spas and massage parlors in my area are small, one-story cement or brick buildings with a steel door...and crappy signs. It may appear as though nobody is there, when in fact, many park their vehicles in an adjacent lot and enter through the back door.

Take-aways

- There are many different types of labor trafficking.
- Labor trafficking is most common in geographic regions where the economy is poor, violence, war or natural disasters have occurred, there is a lack of employment, or a lack of opportunity.

CHAPTER 6

In Plain Site

More than 70% of all runaways encounter a child predator within the first 48 hours of leaving home. Due to the increase of internet access, we have seen a drastic drop in the amount of time between a child running away, or being thrown out, and a trafficker finding them. Many children have access to social media and will leave messages for all to see that they will be leaving home or have just left home. It does not take long for a trafficker to show up as the "rescuer."

Predators/traffickers know what to look for when it comes to vulnerabilities in people. Partly because many of them have the lived the kind of life they are now looking to exploit, and partly because they are intelligent observers of human behavior. Predators/traffickers know if an individual is worth pursuing based on how a person walks; responds to simple questions; if eye contact is made; or if they appear hungry, thirsty, or tired. They also can identify those who are homeless and in need of a place to sleep. Some of the indicators include: if someone is carrying all of their belongings in a garbage bag, wearing more than one set of clothing, or not wearing enough clothes for the weather. A trafficker knows within eight minutes if they have a victim of sex trafficking on the hook (MSP, 2018).

Example

A couple of years ago, my daughter and I encountered a situation at our local gym. We had planned out our regular day at the gym and picked up my daughter's friend on the way. My daughter and her friend were fifteen-years old at the time. I should preface this with the fact that our local gym is located within a large shopping mall. There are entrances on the outside and the inside of the mall. Two of its walls are glass and the people walking in the mall can see people working out inside the gym and the people inside in the gym can see out into the mall area. When we arrived at the gym and I parked my minivan, I noticed there was a young man sitting just outside the entrance to the gym and the mall. When my daughter and her friend got out of the car, this man looked at them and jumped up as if very excited to see them. I went into instant "Mother Bear" mode and stared him down. FYI, your first line of defense is to stare down the threat, take it all in. I made sure this man knew I saw him and could pick him out of a line-up. I quickly took an assessment of his tall, skinny frame; his green and white track suit; his skin color; facial hair; hair style; and tattoos.

The man then went in the mall entrance and the girls and I went into the gym entrance. After a few minutes, I decided to let the girls do their own thing and they shuffled to the tread-mills. I noticed the man once again. This time he was on the other side of the glass, pacing the wall near the treadmills. He was clearly taking notice of my daughter and her friend. He had his cell phone out and was texting most of the time. After a few minutes of observing his unnatural interest in my girls, I began to approach the girls to warn them, but I was beaten to the punch by a police officer working out in a different section of the gym. She ran up to the girls and said, "I don't mean to scare you, but that guy is scoping you out." I was stunned! I was also super grateful that someone other than Mom had told them of the danger. Far too often, my kids do not heed my warnings, but will if the warning comes from a different, but credible source. The police officer and I talked for a bit and continued to observe this young man's behavior. Every few minutes, he would get visibly excited and notice a young girl enter the mall. He would then get really close to her and follow her for a few seconds. I am not sure if he was asking her a question or simply testing her reaction to his physical closeness, but he was definitely testing for vulnerabilities. He would them back off and get back on his phone.

The game this man was playing is typical of many traffick-ers. You see, this man was not alone. He was texting a partner at a different part of the mall, giving the descriptions of po-tential victims; what they looked like, what store they went in, etc. They were both part of a sex trafficking ring. It was not their intention or plan to drug and carry girls out of the mall. Their game was much more sophisticated. The man receiv-ing the texts of potential victims would find them in the mall and casually bump into them. He would then tell them how pretty they were and ask seemingly benign questions about what they were doing at the mall. For instance, "What are buying here today?" "Are you going to get lunch?" You get the idea. The trafficker then might ask if he can buy her a pretzel or something to drink, or simply ask if he can "friend" her on Snapchat, Instagram, Facebook, or some other app. The interaction may seem innocent enough, but in a few days, the trafficker will ask if she would like to go to a party or meet up somewhere. And, when she agrees, it's all over; the grooming process is in full effect.

Take-away

- Predators know exactly how to identify vulnerabilities in individuals, particularly those who have been previously abused.

CHAPTER 7

Demand

The big question remains...Why does human trafficking exist and persist?

The simple answer is, DEMAND! If no one were in the business of purchasing cheap labor or sex, no one would be supplying. Three primary components of demand are the men who purchase sex acts (in any of the commercial sex forms); the traffickers who make up the sex and labor industry; and the culture that puts up with or even promotes sexual and labor exploitation (Gerassi, 2015). Other factors that play into the issue of human trafficking include: increased globalization, gender inequalities, lack of accountability for pimps (suppliers) and johns (buyers), lack of services for victims once they are rescued, ease of mobility, and easy access to pornography.

Today, more than any other time in history, people have the capacity to talk to people anywhere in the world. I know we like to think we live in the day and age of equal rights and feminism, but the truth remains that we live in a nation where large groups of one gender continue to dehumanize the other through rape, violence, or turning a blind eye. We cannot ignore that most johns are men, and the majority of victims are female and children. That is not to say that women do not buy sex or produce pornography, because they do. That is not to say that little boys and men are not exploited and raped, they are. But, we have to take a deep hard look at how gender roles play a part in the issue of sex trafficking here in the United States. Cultural dynamics of how men and women are perceived and received by their own cohort and by the opposite gender, plays a big role in why this nation continues to fuel a culture of rape, violence, and the notion that sex should be violent and violence is sexy.

Lack of accountability for pimps and johns has been an on-going struggle for law enforcement and victims. The motives for pimps and johns are often different. Pimps, or traffickers, are in the business of making money. They lure, trap, and exploit individuals for the purpose of making a lot of money, and they do. Traffickers are often drawn into the business of slave ownership, because the risks are low and the rewards are very high. Traffickers can easily become millionaires by controlling people's lives through drugs, violence, rape, blackmail, etc. Johns, more often than not, rape children and purchase sex for the feeling of power (Shared Hope International, 2011). One-third of all johns were aware the children and women they were paying for sex were being forced, tricked, or lured into trafficking (9 Reasons Why Men Solicit, 2018). They were also aware that many of those being prostituted were underage when they began. Neither of these of factors deterred johns from purchasing sex from women and children. Most johns have wives, girlfriends, family, friends, and jobs. Most johns reported they purchased sex for the thrill of having someone submit. An imbalance of power was a determining factor. They also reported they wanted the "porn" experience; rape, violence, torture, and role play. Johns also said they purchased sex because they wanted to do the kinds of "dirty" sex acts that their wives and girlfriends would not do. Johns reported they had not started out purchasing sex, but rather, viewing pornography. The progression of addiction, escalation, normalizing, and then acting out sexually was the common path that led to purchasing sex.

In some states, pornography has actually been identified as a health crisis. Viewing pornography on a regular basis changes the way the brain operates and is comparable to a drug addiction. Approximately 70% of all men and about 40% of women, view pornography on a regular basis. The progression of viewing pornography to acting out sexually may take a long time or a very short period of time. This is not to say that all those who view pornography go through the progression from viewing to acting out, but most johns who purchase sex have gone through this process.

For many years, men who have participated in the buying and selling of sex have been looked at as just "getting their needs met" or "boys will be boys." This is not the way it should be, but from the beginning of time, it has been. There must be a shift in the thinking of men, boys, women, and girls that reflect the needs and value of all people. We must continue to educate one another on the atrocities of human trafficking and come up with creative ways to intervene in the lives of those most vulnerable in order to prevent human trafficking from occurring. More than 85% of johns said they would be deterred from purchasing sex if the consequences included being put on the sex offender registry and/or having their name and photo posted in public places (social media, billboards, etc.) (Shared Hope International, 2011).

We get several calls a year for girls, boys, women, and men who need services. Some need counseling, while others need an immediate escape from their captors, but the lack of available services makes it very difficult to help in any significant or long-term way.

The increased amount and access to pornography has skyrocketed. There is a book called Epidemic: America's Trade in Child Rape, written by Lori Handrahan. It reviews the horrific data surrounding child pornography, rape and violence, and why it continues to persist. Her research indicates that the rate of infant and toddler rape and use in pornography is sharply on the rise. More than 25 million images of child pornography are reviewed by the National Center for Missing and Exploited Children, each year (2017).

Take-aways

- There are three things needed for trafficking to occur in any area: those willing to exploit the vulnerable, those willing to abuse and buy, and a culture willing to accept it.

- The motives of traffickers (suppliers) and johns (buyers) are different but equally heinous.
- Johns report the beginning of their degradation into abusing children and paying for sex acts began with pornography.
- Pornography has been identified as a public health crisis in some states.

CHAPTER 8

Social Media

Social media plays a significant role in the process of recruiting and grooming victims. The internet provides the means for traffickers to sell and trade children and adults for sexual purposes. Approximately 70% of those sold into sex trafficking are sold through online platforms like Craigslist and the former website, Backpage (Dr. Dominique Roe-Sepowitz, et al., 2017). One in five children, ages 10-17, report they have been approached by an online predator (Social Judo, 2017). Traffickers who once recruited victims in person, have turned to the internet for easy access and grooming. Promises of modeling jobs, recording contacts, or simply offering a listening ear are common recruiting techniques used to lure children into "the game."

A recent policy change has made it more difficult for traffickers to post advertisements to online platforms like Craigslist and the former Backpage (Jackman, 2017). After a lawsuit was filed by a couple of mothers whose daughters had been sold through Backpage.com, the Federal Court system became involved and created policy to help deter online platform holders from allowing traffickers to post advertisements on their sites. For more information on the court process involving this case, look up the documentary, "I am Jane Doe." In short, Backpage.com executives successfully argued they were not responsible for what third-parties posted as they were merely the holder of the internet space. The law they hid behind is the Communications Decency Act of 1994. The original law was updated when two new laws were created; the FOSTA (Fight Online Sex Trafficking Act) and the SESTA (Stop Enabling Sex Trafficking Act). These new laws were signed in by President Trump in April 2018. FOSTA states that if anyone is found to be "knowingly assisting, supporting or facilitating a violation," they can be brought up on civil charges through the State Attorney General's office and held criminally liable and financially responsible.

The shutting down of Backpage.com was a great win. It did however create some challenges for law enforcement because it was the biggest resource for finding victims of sex trafficking (Guirguis, 2018). Traffickers may have been slowed for a moment, but it did not take long for them to move ads to other social media sites, apps, and chat rooms. There is no shortage of platforms, more than 15,000 new apps created each week and Facebook has become one of the primary mediums for trafficking.

Many children and adults who are on social media and the internet have no idea how to identify a predator and can get swept away by feelings, not thinking logically about the interactions occurring in front of them (Social Judo, 2017).

Approximately 83-95% of all teens in the United States have a Facebook account and have an average of 425 FB friends. Most people are not aware that one in every 50 profiles on Facebook is fake!

Some warning signs of online predators can include:

- Having no friends in common with you
- Having a very common first and last name, (Richard Jones, Mary Smith, John Downs are just a few examples of requests I have received and were fake profiles). Sometimes their names are misspelled. If you click on their page and discover that most of what they type is misspelled or spelled phonetically, this can be an indication that English is not their first language.
- If their profile picture or other pictures are low quality (grainy), this could be a clue that the photo was downloaded from someone else's page, Google, or some other internet site.
- Predators will often use your "about" section and your noted interests to create their profile, making it appear as though you both have the same or similar interests, hobbies, or careers.
- And if today was the magic day they decided to create a Facebook page and YOU are their first friend, yet you do not know who they are, something is definitely amiss.

Example

Recently I received a message, not a friend request and not from someone who was already a friend, just a message...from 'Sam Smith', not the singer. He started the conversation with "Hey, how are you? What's going on today?" I was intrigued. I had just completed a very large seminar and thought, 'I wonder if he was in the seminar yesterday?' I asked him if I had met him before or if he was in the group I had just taught, and he said "No, I came across your profile pic and you look really pretty. I thought we could meet for coffee in the Detroit area tomorrow." Well, now I knew something was up. First, I do not live in the 'Detroit area' and those who do, generally don't call it the 'Detroit area.'

Doing what I do, I knew that Sam was a predator. I didn't know yet what kind, so I figured I would ask a few more questions. I quickly went to Sam's profile on Facebook and found he had only 5 friends, and get this, lived in Canada. I quickly returned fire and said "well, Sam, turns out we don't even live in the same country." To which he replied, "it only takes me an hour and half to get to the Detroit area and I will be there tomorrow on business." Being the curious person I am, I asked him what he did for a living and he gave me some long explanation about investments and marketing, and blah blah blah. He then asked me what my job was, so I told him. Needless to say, Sam never responded and quickly disappeared from my radar. Turns out when you train others to spot sexual predators, the predators generally steer clear.

If you find yourself, or someone you know, faced with a predator, the first thing you should do is report their account to Facebook, or whatever social media platform you are using. There is an option to report when a friend request is sent, you should utilize an option to report whenever you feel the profile you are viewing was created under false pretense. Then, block the user from sending you any additional requests. This too can usually be done right through your account settings page. This is also where you will find different options for privacy. It is suggested you set your privacy to "private" or "friends only" to protect yourself from receiving unwanted friend requests.

Be aware and alert of any changes in your friends, or family members' behavior. Often, it is friends or family who recognize when someone is being targeted by a predator or trafficker. Whenever I speak to groups of adolescents, there is usually a report of human trafficking and/or sexual abuse immediately following. Every time we have received a report, it was reported by a friend of the person it was happening to, and not the person themselves. Victims often do not see the hell they are trapped in, but friends do!

Never post ANYTHING on-line that you would not want posted on a freeway billboard. Once photos, videos, and statements are shared, they are out there forever. There are some apps that claim to erase all messages, videos, and pictures after a certain period of time, but they do not permanently disappear. They remain stored in an internet-based cloud platform, FOREVER! Be careful what you post!

There are ways to protect you, your loved ones, and your workplace. Companies like Covenant Eyes in Michigan and NetClean, provide software for the whole family and the workplace. For more information visit their websites at www.netclean.com and www.covenanteyes.com.

Take-aways

- Social media plays an enormous role in the recruitment, grooming, and selling of sex trafficking victims.
- Approximately 70% of sex trafficking victims are sold through online platforms.
- Knowing the signs of predators online can save lives.
- Never post anything online that you do not want out in the internet world, FOREVER!
- Friends of victims are often the ones reporting suspicious behavior.

CHAPTER 9

Predators/Traffickers

So, what does a trafficker look like? Do you think you can tell just by looking at someone? Perhaps it would be easier if they all wore uniforms. If they all wore tall colorful hats, long fur coats, and used a gold-tipped walking cane for decoration, we would definitely be at an advantage. Unfortunately, that is not the case, unless it is Halloween.

The truth is, you don't know who a trafficker or predator is simply by looking at them. It is not indicated by the clothes they wear or anything thing else. They look just like you and me; every color, age, gender, culture, and creed.

We used to have a game we would play during seminars called Keeper or Creeper (I know, not very politically correct but bear with me). We would put photos of a dozen individuals of varying ages, races, and gender, then ask all the participants to agree on whether they thought the person in the photo was a Keeper or a Creeper. Inevitably, by the end, all the participants thought everyone shown was a creeper. They were so wrong. I had a couple pictures of family members and other friends of mine and they were definitely NOT creepers. It was a great visual example of how you cannot tell if someone is a predator based solely on appearances.

Sex traffickers are often hiding in plain sight. They have jobs, families, friends, and often hold positions of authority within their own community (Dr. Dominique Roe-Sepowitz, et al., 2017). Of 88 sex traffickers identified and reported upon, 28 ran their own business or held a position in the private or service industry (taxi or truck drivers, repair persons, etc.), 22 were identified as rap artists, 16 held positions of authority (police officers, counselors, and security guards), 10 had direct access to children through their occupation (elementary schools, group homes for trouble youth, and one juvenile probation officer), Nine sex traffickers were already running or working in legal sex industry markets (dancing, strip clubs), Eight were public figures, Seven were in law enforcement, Six were in the military, Five were students, Three worked at hotels and Two worked in schools.

Myths and Truths About Traffickers/Predators

Myth #1 – They are always men.
Truth – About half of all recruiters for human trafficking in the United States are women and girls (Dr. Dominique Roe-Sepowitz, et al., 2017). Many mothers, grand-mothers, aunts, and other women take part in the production and distribution of child pornography, and many also run residential

brothels. While the majority of traffickers, predators, and pedophiles are males, it does not make women exempt from the same activities.

Myth #2 – They are always old and creepy.

Truth – We often have a visual of older men preying on young children and women, but the truth is that the average rapist is 31 years old and the average age of a trafficker is 28.5 years old (ASU Research).

Myth #3 – They are dumb.

Truth – Many traffickers are so intelligent they could be CEOs of major corporations. Many know how to navigate the "deep web," an intricate internet system that scrambles IPOs and bounces from one internet platform to another. Some traffickers network with others and discuss how best to buy, sell, transport, and harbor human beings for nefarious purposes.

Myth #4 – They are loners.

Truth – Most buyers and sellers of human beings have family and friends, go to work or school, and have a social life. The truth is, most 'dates' that are made through the internet (the purchase of sex through online platforms) are done between the hours of 2 and 4 pm, from a work computer (MI State Troopers, conference 2017).

Myth #5 – Traffickers choose strangers to kidnap and violate.

Truth – Less than 3% of those trafficked in the United

States were kidnapped. Most victims of trafficking know their captor. It could be a family member, friend, or acquaintance (MSP, 2017). In a study conducted by Arizona State University, only 7.8% of those trafficked for sexual purposes, were exploited by complete strangers (Dr. Dominique Roe-Sepowitz, et al., 2017).

The Way In

Understanding the grooming process is an important step in identifying and responding to human trafficking. Grooming is the process during which a sexual predator draws a person in, usually a child or adolescent, by gaining his or her trust in order to exploit them for sex, labor, or both.

Traffickers and sexual predators know exactly what kinds of human behaviors indicate vulnerabilities (The Victims and Traffickers, 2017). They often look for emotional neediness, isolation, low self-esteem, and lack of parental attention. These vulnerabilities may be indicated by a child or adult through an online platform or in person. Predators know based on how someone walks, talks, the way they look (or don't look) at you, or how they respond to a question; how easy it will be to trick, lure, coerce, or force into trafficking. It only takes about eight minutes for a trafficker to know if they have a victim on the hook. Traffickers will often spend weeks, even months, grooming and manipulating their way into someone's psyche because trafficking humans is where the money is. Human beings can be sold over and over again, so the amount of time invested is seen as a necessary business tool.

- Most johns have jobs, spouses, children, and friends.
- Some myths about trafficker are that they are always men, old, creepy, dumb, alone, and strangers to their victims.
- Traffickers are skilled at identifying vulnerabilities.
- The grooming process includes targeting victims, gaining the victim's need, filling a need, isolating the victim, sexualizing interactions, and maintaining control.

CHAPTER 10

Warning Signs

Common warning signs in medical, mental health, and education settings.

Survivors of sex trafficking, in the United States, reported these statistics (Syme, RDH, MS, 2017):

- During victimization, 26-50% of human trafficking survivors sought medical attention in places such as emergency rooms, dental offices, etc., while they were being trafficked. This means that while individuals were still being bought and sold, they interacted with some kind of medical professional.
- Of those being trafficked, 57% reported physical injury.
- 40% of those injuries were caused by weapons or instruments. The use of violence and rape are often used to maintain control and can cause serious physical and psychological harm to victims.
- Sexual and physical assault was reported by 95% of victims. The only reason I can think of that this number is not 100% is because this a self-reporting study and

victim of trafficking often do not self-identify as victims. They often believe they have chosen this life, or somehow deserve what they get. They do not understand that they have been targeted, groomed, and are now trapped.

The top presenting complaints to medical personnel during victimization include:

- back pain
- headaches
- gastrointestinal problems (stomach aches, diarrhea, constipation, etc.)
- fractures
- contusions (bruises)
- burns
- dental complaints
- vaginal bleeding
- pelvic pain
- retained foreign objects in rectum or vagina

Back, stomach, and head pain is often associated with psychological trauma showing up in the body (Pinaki Mukherji, 2015). Pain may be present without any medical explanation and often requires practitioners to take a thorough history of experienced trauma. This will allow them to fully assess the cause and treatment of symptoms.

Specifically for those in the dental field (Syme, RDH, MS,

2017), while treating folks who may be victims of human trafficking, there are some tell-tale indicators to look for. You are going to look for broken teeth, broken or dislocated jaw, sexually transmitted infections, and/or very poor oral health. It is helpful to have some form of policy in place to help victims, or anybody who struggles with dental procedures, to help identify triggers and diminish anxiety while in treatment. If a patient appears to be very nervous, address safety concerns first. Ask if they are safe at home or with the person who brought them (if they came with someone else). If they feel they are in immediate danger, call the appropriate authorities to help the patient.

Victims of sex trafficking may present with sexually transmitted infections, unwanted pregnancy (sometimes a victim has tried to perform an at-home abortion or someone else has tried to do it to them and they end up in the emergency room). Mental health complications are almost inevitable when it comes to victims of trauma and may present with symptoms of anxiety, depression, and suicidal ideation. Approximately 90% of those trafficked have a substance abuse issue. It is often used as a means of control and create dependency on the trafficker.

Things to watch out for when interacting with a potential victim of human trafficking are:

- Repeated injuries over time, resulting in scarring and poorly care for wounds. If someone has bumpy or very thick scar tissue, this could be an indication an injury was not properly tended to, or the injury was repeatedly inflicted on the victim, at the same location on the body.

- Repeated symmetrical injuries; patterns made by bite marks, tools, belts, cords, shoes, or kitchen utensils.
- Linear or circular burns (this is often used as a form of torture, punishment, rite of passage, or branding to indicate ownership).
- Bruising on the cheek, neck, trunk, and buttocks is unusual for accidental injury and should be taken very seriously.
- Tattoos of names, numbers, or barcodes can indicate ownership. There may be several of these, indicating transfer of ownership from one trafficker to another, this is called "trading up" or "trading down."

Warning signs in any setting include:

- If someone is unable to speak for themselves. Someone else is always telling their story for them. This can happen anywhere, in a hospital, doctor's office, resource center, etc.
- They are never alone.
- Not in control of the money they earn.
- Signs of physical or sexual abuse.
- If someone is confused and cannot keep details straight. Some think this is an indication the victim is lying but that is generally not the case. When trauma occurs, memories are stored in the emotional and feeling centers of the brain and language and logic are disengaged.

This leaves many victims unable to tell their story in a logical manner. Often, trauma memories have no logical beginning or end, just a very messy middle. Over time, more details may emerge, giving a false pretense that the story is not true when in fact it is.

- If a victim is unaware of what day it is, what city he or she is in, or what year they were born, that is a huge red flag.
- If they lie about their age. For example, they are 15 years old and say they are 18.
- If someone refers to, usually an older, un-related male as "Daddy" or "Boyfriend" or an un-related female as "Wifey," Wifey-in-law," or "Sister-wives"
- Someone who is unable to come and go freely.
- Working especially long hours, more than more than 10 hours a day and 6 or 7 days per week.
- Receiving little or no pay for work performed.
- Working in harsh conditions. Hard labor conditions with few or no breaks, limited access to water or food, and limits on bathroom use are just a few examples of harsh working conditions.
- Excessive security measure in the work area. If there are gates surrounding a property or house with security cameras outside and inside of the home, but is not consistent with the type of neighborhood, there may be something concerning going on. If you notice frequent visitors, or people coming in and out of the home or facilities at all hours of the day and night, this is also a red flag.
- If a worker or student exhibits an unusual degree of

fear and/or anxiety. Now take this one seriously but If someone is displaying symptoms of PTSD (Post-Traumatic Stress Disorder), hypervigilant, nervousness, etc., talk to them about it. Find out what is happening and go from there.

Common indicators of human trafficking:

- If someone comes from, or lives in, an abusive home.
- Has more than one cell phone.
- Is angry, withdrawn, or depressed. Now, I must put a small disclaimer on this one because often adolescents camp out here but if symptoms are beyond typically occurring developmental stages, then it is cause for concern. If symptoms are present for an extended period or appear to be more extreme than typical for the age and stage of the individual, this should be addressed with the appropriate helping professionals (therapists, nurses, doctors, pastors, etc.).
- If someone, especially a young person, possesses large sums of money. This is generally beyond what would be expected for the type of job and age of person.
- A lack of parental supervision and support
- If someone appears hungry or malnourished
- If they are inappropriately dressed
- Going into high crime areas

Example

When I was in first grade, there were several kids in the house. I do not have a whole lot of memory from that time period, but I do remember getting into a lot of trouble at school. We were never given breakfast, nor were we packed a lunch. I would ask the teacher if I could go to the bathroom, and on the way, grab other kids' lunch boxes, and eat the food once I got to the bathroom. After a while, the school recognized there was an issue, but I don't recall it did much good. We were all very hungry and this was a big glaring sign that something was not right at home. In the 1980's however, most people, including school administration, did not get too involved in family business.

Challenges in identifying victims can include:

- A lack of access to legal or supportive services
- Fear of retaliation from traffickers
- Have been conditioned to fear and distrust anyone other than their captor
- Fear of consequences of being an illegal immigrant or criminal
- Feeling ashamed and fear of rejection from family and community
- Feeling hopeless
- Feeling as though they owe something to their captor, or trafficker. Often, one's trafficker is the first one to show any kindness, providing a place to live, clothing, food, security, etc.
- Victims do not self-identify as victims of human trafficking. Most do not know or understand the termi-

nology, and do not identify as being a victim. Many survivors believe they have chosen the life they are living and do not understand that they were chosen. Nearly 30% do not understand they are being exploited (Landers, McGrath, Johnson, Armstrong, & Dollard, 2017).

Take-aways

- Upwards of half of those trafficked see a medical professional during their victimization.
- Psychosomatic complaints are common among trafficking victims, i.e., back pain, headaches, and gastrointestinal problems.
- Things to watch for include unusual injuries, tattoos, cannot speak for themselves, are young but possess large sums of money, have several cell phones, appear to be afraid, using language associated with sex trafficking and gang activity, and if the victim is confused and cannot keep details straight.
- Some challenges in identifying victims include not having access to local resources, fear of retaliation, and victims not being able to self-identify.

CHAPTER 11

How to Report

If the suspected victim is under the age of 18, your first call is going to be to Child Protective Services, this number will vary from state to state.

Then call the Human Trafficking Hotline at **1-888-3737-888**.

If it is an emergency, regardless of age, you are going to call 911, then the Human Trafficking Hotline.

If the suspected victim is over the age of 18, the victim needs and wants help, you are going to call the Human Trafficking Hotline. If it is safer to text, they may text "help" or "save me" to **233733** or **"BeFree."**

For additional resources go to Polaris Project at www.polarisproject.org, click on the tab that says, "get assistance" and then click on, or type in, your geographic area. Additional resources include the National Center for Missing and Exploited Children, Shared Hope International, and International Justice Mission.

Take-aways

- Report! Report! Report!

CHAPTER 12

Common Threads

Developed from personal interaction and data collection, there are some shared experiences by victims of trafficking that continued to appear. Many victims reported negative early childhood experiences; the leading cause of vulnerabilities in those targeted by traffickers. In 2016, an estimated 676,000 children were victims of abuse and neglect in the United States. According to several studies, 86% to 91% of sex trafficking victims have a history of childhood sexual abuse and one in five runaways are likely victims of sex trafficking (Landers, McGrath, Johnson, Armstrong, & Dollard, 2017) (Polaris Project, 2018).

Vulnerabilities in victims are often created by the following experiences and statuses:

- Foster care
- Runaway / "Throwaway"
- History of abuse
- Substance abuse
- LGBTQ identification

- Homelessness
- Lack of social safety net
- Poverty
- Gender discrimination
- Criminal activity
- Immigration status

Children in the foster care system, experience homelessness, have runaway, and have already been abused at home, are at the greatest risk for being targeted by traffickers and easily fall into a life of sex trafficking (Dr. Dominique Roe-Sepowitz, et al., 2017) (Foster Care & Human Trafficking, 2017). A Six-Year Analysis of Sex Trafficking of Minors (2017) reported in 2015, that nearly 30% of minor sex trafficking victims were foster care children. Children who have aged out of the foster care system and have a history of abuse are more likely to engage in transactional sex (Gerassi, 2015). Non-typically occurring experiences in childhood, i.e. being physically, emotionally, or verbally abused; having one or both parents abuse alcohol or drugs; or the experience of poverty create vulnerabilities in children that carry throughout their adolescents and into adulthood (J. Douglas Bremner, 2006) (Felitti, 2018). The brains of those experiencing trauma can actually become conditioned to seek out and accept the lies and coercion of predators, making it nearly impossible to escape their childhood realities.

Impact of Trauma

Child abuse and neglect has been linked to impaired brain

development, juvenile delinquency, and serious injury and death (Bessel Van Der Kolk, 2014) (Bessel A. Van Der Kolk, 2003) (Felitti, 2018). Other indicators include developmental disabilities, socializing problems, poor school performance, depression and suicide, and teen pregnancy. During traumatic events, the brain sends a signal to either run away, or stay and fight (Department of Health and Human Services, 2015) (Roelofs, 2017). When neither flee or fight is an option, the whole system goes in to shut-down mode and freezes.

Over time, a child who is abused will develop a maladaptive trigger system, alarming the brain to flee, fight, or freeze repeatedly, even if there is little or no threat (Bessel A. Van Der Kolk, 2003) (Department of Health and Human Services, 2015) (Roelofs, 2017). This consistent triggering floods the brain with alarmist chemicals and hormones, most notably adrenaline and cortisol. Without the release of chemicals that bring the brain and body system back to center, or a state of homeostasis, the trigger system is so overactive that even the most benign situation can elicit a full-on traumatic event.

The brain is a complex organ and is designed to keep the entire system (the body) alive at any cost (Monica Bucci, Silverio Marques DrPH, Oh, PhD, MSc, & Burke Harris, MD, MPH, 2016) (Roelofs, 2017) (Seltzer PhD, 2015) (J. Douglas Bremner, 2006). During traumatic events the brain first activates the sympathetic nervous system. This system is designed to get the body ready for action; heart rate increases, blood pressure rises, and the body gets ready to either run (flee) or fight. When fleeing or fighting is not an option, usually because the threat is much bigger, stronger, or poses a fatal threat (being held at gunpoint), the parasympathetic nervous system becomes active. This response is often referred to as "playing opossum," the brain shuts down parts of the system, getting it ready to play dead until the threat has passed. Some of the affected areas are the Broca's area, hippocampus, amygdala, and prefrontal cortex (Bessel A. Van Der Kolk, 2003).

The Broca's area, or language center of the brain, has little or no activity during trauma (Bessel A. Van Der Kolk, 2003) (Bessel Van Der Kolk, 2014). If you have ever witnessed someone who has just gone through a horrible event and could not speak, it is because they literally had no words. It is not difficult to understand why victims of sexual abuse cannot tell their story.

The hippocampus begins to die off and shrink (Bessel Van Der Kolk, 2014). The hippocampus is partially responsible for properly processing and storing memory, as well as memory recall. The ability to learn new information becomes very difficult when this portion of the brain does not function appropriately (Roelofs, 2017). Impact on the amygdala is equally disturbing. The amygdala is the emotional center of the brain and becomes overactive when repeated trauma triggers flight, fight, or freeze and there is diminished growth in the prefrontal cortex; the area responsible for executive decision-making, impulse control, and problem-solving (Monica Bucci, Silverio Marques DrPH, Oh, PhD, MSc, & Burke Harris, MD, MPH, 2016). Trauma, over time, results in poor memory recall; dissociation; personality disorders; depression;

anxiety, complex post-traumatic stress disorder; Stockholm Syndrome; substance abuse; diabetes; heart disease; somatic syndrome; and a myriad of other disorders and diseases.

Maslow's Hierarchy of Needs (1943) has been a long-standing guide for those in the social work world. Abraham Maslow's description of what it takes to survive and thrive as a healthy individual from the most basic needs to the most complex, yet still very necessary, is a simple guide of what it takes survive and thrive. Working our way from the bottom to the top, *physical needs* must be met first. These are the things we all must have if we are to survive; food, water, and sleep. Then comes safety, not just physical safety but mental and emotional safety. For example, a thirteen-year old is kicked out her home in the winter, in the middle of a city with no so-cial support and has not eaten anything in two days, her first priority is to get something to eat and she does not give a rip about safety until her physical need is met. Once fed, shel-tered, clothed, etc., she will be in search of safety; physical, emotional, and mental safety. This is where many victims of human trafficking and on-going trauma get stuck; their lives become a never-ending loop of getting physical needs met and searching for safety.

Once *physical* and *safety* needs are attended to and one is confident they can remain in these states for a substantial period of time, one seeks and moves on to *love and belonging*. The word "belonging" itself has become a bit of buzzword in recent years. Science and religion alike, agree that belonging plays an essential role in physical, emotional, and mental well-being (Brown). Belonging to a group of friends, family, or community allow individuals to create safety and confidence; it gives meaning and purpose to interactions with others.

Once individuals feel as if they safely belong, they move on to *esteem*; a desire to be valued and respected by others and ourselves. And then, finally, *self-actualization*, which essentially means "I know who I am, I know what direction I am headed, and I kind of like myself."

Many of us bounce between the top two tiers because let's be honest, some days we wake up and are like "ah, you're crap", "you shouldn't have done _____" or "you're such a loser." Some days are just harder than others and it's enough to just eat, sleep, and feel safe in our own homes.

While many of us do struggle with bouncing around this pyramid, for the most part, we are okay and can navigate life, friends, family, and ourselves pretty well. But, when someone has encountered evil, has lived a life of trauma after trauma, and simply knows no other way, they tend to bounce only between the bottom two tiers. Constantly searching for food, shelter, and safety are priority, and if they are lucky, receive a bit of attention. It is sad to say that many have not experienced much beyond basic needs and safety and when a trafficker comes along to offer love and attention, some of those needs that have never been addressed begin to be met. Sometimes, the closest thing to love victims will ever experience is from their trafficker. It is not hard to understand why it is difficult for victims of trafficking to get out of "the life" and stay out. The trafficker filled needs that nobody else did; creating *trauma bonds* (Stockholm Syndrome) that are very difficult to break.

Mental Health Diagnoses

Top presenting mental health disorders associated with those who have been abused over time, including those who have been trafficked, are Post-Traumatic Stress Disorder, Depression, Anxiety, Stockholm Syndrome (trauma bonds), and Dissociation (Bessel A. Van Der Kolk, 2003) (Felitti, 2018) (Landers, McGrath, Johnson, Armstrong, & Dollard, 2017) (Sartory, et al., 2013). Every diagnosis, disorder, disease, and maladaptation are different depending on the victim's personality, resilience, and severity of trauma. No diagnosis should be looked as a cookie-cutter explanation for how someone should or shouldn't respond to adverse events. The aforementioned complications are not exhaustive, there are a whole host of additional symptoms and diagnoses attributed to victims of trauma and on-going abuse. Some of those additional diagnoses might include, Substance Abuse, Attention Deficit Disorder (with or without Hyperactivity), Eating Disorders, Personality Disorders, Oppositional Defiant Disorder, Reactive Attachment Disorder, and the list goes on (Felitti, 2018) (Landers, McGrath, Johnson, Armstrong, & Dollard, 2017) (The Blue Knock Foundation, 2018).

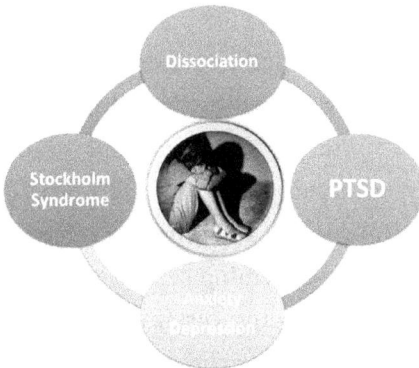

Stockholm Syndrome

Every now and again, there is a news report of another girl or woman who had been taken and held captive but did not take opportunities to leave or seek help. Trauma bonding or Stockholm Syndrome is a well-documented phenomenon where captive victims develop psychological attachments to their captor (Dr. Dominique Roe-Sepowitz, et al., 2017). This a survival mechanism and allows the victim to be able to endure the manipulation, torture, and entrapment common in trafficking situations. Stockholm Syndrome, like many other disorders, exists on a spectrum to "I kind of feel bad for him" to "I will die for him. I will do whatever it takes to protect him and will never tell." It is an extreme and seemingly unnatural bond with one's captor/trafficker, but make no mistake, it is survival.

Post-Traumatic Stress Disorder

PTSD (Post-Traumatic Stress Disorder) includes varying degrees of disturbing thoughts, flashbacks, body memories, triggering events, startle responses, and so on (Lundberg, 2016) (Sartory, et al., 2013). It is often characterized by a search for environmental and internal safety; i.e. scanning one's surroundings, performing certain tasks (locking doors, shutting oneself in, avoiding certain people or places, etc.). Symptoms may also include difficulty with attachment; biological problems such as sensory integration problems, changes to the brain, and an increased risk of developing auto-immune disorders; damage to executive functioning; dissociation including Dissociative Identity Disorder; difficulties with impulse control, aggression, self-harming behavior, and sleep disturbances; problems with emotional regulation; and a disturbing self-concept that results in body image problems, low self-worth, and excessive shame.

Depression

Depression often has behaviors associated with feeling "down," lethargic, loss of interest in things that were once interesting, not wanting to be around people, sleeping too much or not enough, changes in appetite (eating too much or not enough), feeling bad about oneself, difficulty concentrating, and thoughts of hurting oneself or suicidal ideation.

Anxiety

Symptoms of anxiety include a state of uneasiness, apprehension, uncertainty, and/or fear about a real or perceived threat. Anxiety, or panic attacks, can include tightness in the chest, tingling fingers and toes, dizziness, headaches, stomach upset, pulsing in the ear, inability to relax, feeling like you are going crazy, and sleep disturbances. There are many more symptoms that can be listed here but you get the idea.

Dissociation

Dissociative disorders, like the others, exists on a spectrum. It can include feeling like one is not attached to their body or being in a "floaty" kind of state, to having several different personalities; created to take on unbearable trauma (Bessel Van Der Kolk, 2014) (Felitti, 2018). Characteristics include feeling disconnected from one's body; memory loss of certain time periods, events, people and personal information; a sense that people and things are not real or distorted; rapids changes in mood; and others.

Tips to help with dissociative symptoms are to first, develop an awareness of what triggers exist, so they can be prevented. Two, notice when dissociative episodes are coming on, and three, develop a list of strategies to prevent or interrupt the episode. Some strategies or tips include: use tactile sensations to keep your mind and body untied; tough rough surfaces or run your hands under cold water; go outside where your senses are more fully engaged, focus on feeling the wind on your face or touching the bark of a tree; and get involved in some physical activity.

Warning Signs in Children of Abuse

While it is imperative to understand the dynamics involved with human trafficking, it is doubly important to recognize when someone is being abused and exploited. It does no good to talk of the stats and stories if we cannot identify the warning signs of current abuse. Whether you are a professional who works with children or a concerned family member, your children need you!

Signs of past or current abuse/trafficking

- Persistent stomach aches or headaches
- Bed wetting or other accidents that are not age appro-

priate for development or explained by a medical condition
- Withholding stools
- Hyper-vigilance or inability to sleep
- Overly reclusive or submissive
- Sexually aggressive toward younger child or sexual activities with peers
- Coming to school and other activities early, and not wanting to go home.
- Not receiving attention for physical problems that have been brought to a caregiver's attention.

Take-aways

- Children who have experienced previous abuse, been in the foster care system, are runaways, homelessness, substance abuse, poverty, and being part of the LGBTQ community are top indicators for children at "high risk" for being trafficked.
- The impact of on-going trauma has life-long implications.
- Brain development during trauma can create mental illness, developmental disabilities, medical problems, and even early death.
- Trauma, over time, often is diagnosed later as Complex Post-Traumatic Stress Disorder, Anxiety, Depression, Stockholm Syndrome (Trauma Bonds), and Dissociation.

CHAPTER 13

Adverse Childhood
Experiences Study
(ACE's)

"In my beginning, is my end" ~ ACE study participant

The Adverse Childhood Study began in the 1980s with a group of researchers, through Kaiser Permanente, who stumbled upon common childhood experiences that had direct impact on the health, well-being, and life expectancy of those trying to lose weight and quit smoking. Dr. Vincent Felitti and his team embarked upon a massive research project that involved 17,337 participants through the course of 20 years.

The first discovery of a possible link between obesity and adverse childhood experiences was with a 28-year-old woman. Over 400 pounds, she came to the clinic for help with weight loss. She had tremendous success and lost a significant amount of weight over the course of a year. However, with one sexual comment from a man, the weight drastically piled on. Within three weeks, she had packed on an impressive 37 pounds. Within the year, she was back over 400 pounds. This young woman was a thin, healthy child until the age of 11, precisely the time she began being molested by her grandfather. The researchers began asking other participants about their childhood experiences and found a direct relationship to their health in adulthood.

Weight gain, smoking, drug use, and other behaviors that create health problems are symptoms of a more insidious monster; adverse childhood experiences. Through self-destructive behavior, participants found ways to cope with the trauma they had gone through in their early years. Ten areas of childhood experiences were developed and put to the test with more than 17,000 individuals. The ten areas included if one has been sexually, physically, or verbally abused; neglected; someone in the household has gone to prison; if parents divorced; if someone had a drug or alcohol problem. You get the idea. The higher the score, the greater the risk in adulthood for poor health, mental illness, and early death.

"We are not treating the problem, but someone else's solution" ~ Dr. Felitti.

Dr. Felitti explained it this way. Let us say that someone sees smoke coming out of the windows of a house. The smoke is the symptom of the actual problem, a fire. So too is weight gain, smoking cigarettes, using street drugs, and all other coping methods a symptom of the real problem; unresolved adverse childhood experiences. Instead of addressing only the symptoms, with medication, therapy, etc., there should be a much greater focus on addressing the cause of the symptoms.

Through the first several cases done through Kaiser Permanente, researchers were able to connect adverse childhood experiences to addiction, mental illness, poor health, and most astonishing; suicide. Those who score four or more on the ACE's questionnaire are 5000% times more likely to commit suicide than those who scored a zero. Adverse Childhood Experiences also determine the ten most common causes of death in the United States.

What does the ACE's study have to do with human trafficking? Great question! Those who are targeted and groomed the most for sex trafficking, here in the United States and other well-industrialized nations, have experienced at least four adverse childhood experiences. Children in foster care are in foster care for a reason. Most often they have been sexually and physically abused; have a parent who has a drug or alcohol addiction; and one-third have at least one parent who is deceased (Dr. Dominique Roe-Sepowitz, et al., 2017). Childhood trauma has a direct relationship to human trafficking by creating vulnerabilities, targeted by traffickers.

Suggestions by Dr. Felitti (2018) to help mitigate the effects from adverse childhood experiences are to begin implementing an ACE questionnaire in medical and mental health facilities; explore autobiographical journaling; and hypnosis. The use of ACE's questionnaire reduced the number of doctor office visits, within one year, from study participants, by

35%. Resiliency is not an area that has been studied thoroughly but should be taken into consideration when working with people who have experienced on-going trauma. The human spirit is one that cannot be underestimated, nor adequately studied in a laboratory.

EARLY DEATH

DISEASE,
DISABILITY, &
SOCIAL PROBLEMS

SOCIAL, EMOTIONAL, &
COGNITIVE IMPAIRMENT

DISRUPTED NEURODEVELOPMENT

ADVERSE CHILDHOOD EXPERIENCES

MECHANISM BY WHICH ADVERSE CHILDHOOD EXPERIENCES INFLUENCE HEALTH AND WELL-BEING THROUGOUT THE LIFESPAN

Take-aways

- Adverse childhood experiences are common but generally overlooked or not recognized.
- The link between ACEs and major medical and mental

health problems in adulthood, are strong, proportional, and logical.

- ACEs are the most basic public health problem.
- What often presents as the symptom or the problem, may be a patient's attempted solution.

CHAPTER 14

Healing & Intervention Techniques

There is hope!

Intervention can be scary but is very necessary when faced with a suspected case of human trafficking. It is imperative to create a safe, non-judgmental space. Victims, or suspected victims, need to know first, they are physically safe. This is not to say that you throw common sense out the window. Please do not put yourself between a trafficker and a victim if you feel your safety is in question. If possible, ask the suspected victim if she or he is safe.

If the suspected victim comes in with their suspected trafficker, your first task is to find a way to separate the two. Your company may already have a policy that helps with this step. Some agencies have policies that include conducting separate interviews to receive services. Interview both suspected victim and trafficker, being sure not to let on you suspect there is an issue. Treat both with dignity and respect.

- Communicate in relatable terms. There is a list of common terminology used by traffickers and trafficking victims, at the back of this book. If someone begins to speak to you and you are able to recognize the language, you are a step ahead of the rest. Communicate this language back to the suspected victim. Do not be afraid to ask the victim for clarification if you do not understand something. Do not pretend you have been in "the life" if you have not, people know when someone is not being authentic.
- Develop a rapport with the suspected victim by asking about evident injury, scars, tattoos, and acknowledge symptoms of trauma.
- Attend to safety needs. You will not be able to carry on a meaningful conversation if the suspected victim does not feel safe. Ask them if they feel comfortable opening up and if not, what will help them talk to you.
- Ask about likes, dislikes, and interests; use strengths to draw out conversation; and thank them for having the courage to come to you or open up to you.
- Dig a little deeper by asking open-ended questions. Asking questions that result in a "yes" or "no" may not be very helpful and may bring the conversation to an abrupt end.

Encourage the suspected victim to self-report to the appropriate agency, if they are over the age of 18. If the suspected victim is over the age of 18 and able to make the phone call to get assistance, they are more likely to follow through. If they are unable or unwilling to call and want help, make the call for them!

This is very important: Do NOT let them use their own cell phone. Let them use yours or a landline. Cell phones are often monitored by traffickers and victims will be in danger if they attempt to access help with a tracked device.

If there is time, build trust and rapport through the methods discussed. If there is limited time, jump right to the assessment questions; in the appendix of this book. This downloadable resource will help you determine what steps are needed next. It gives you a starting point in regard to safety issues, sex trafficking, labor trafficking, and debt bondage.

Validate and listen.

The first thing a victim or suspected victim needs to hear from you is "I believe you". They may tell you some horrible, nasty, and unbelievable things, but some people **do** horrible, nasty, and unbelievable things to children and adults. Reflect back to them what they are saying. Make sure they know you really hear them.

Therapeutic Interventions

Combining additional therapeutic interventions with psychodynamic talk-therapy has been proven to help victims of trauma make connections between brain and body, and thereby helping the whole system (the person) heal more effectively and efficiently. Auxiliary therapeutic interventions include, restorative yoga, expressive therapies, mindfulness, and sensory-based practices.

Using strengths, likes, hobbies, spirituality, and interests are essential components to successful healing and restoration of sex trafficking victims (Landers, McGrath, Johnson, Armstrong, & Dollard, 2017). The ability to express their thoughts and emotions, in various ways, only improves their chances for surviving and thriving in an adult world. Resiliency (internal strengths) and resourcefulness (external strengths) are necessary for continued growth and healing.

Restorative yoga has several benefits for the mind and body. Particularly for those who have trouble with dissociation, restorative yoga helps to create a connection between brain and body (Bessel Van Der Kolk, 2014) (Fay, 2017). The process is yoga with some adjustments. It involves yoga poses being held for 5-15 minutes with the support of blankets, towels, blocks, etc. The instructor is specialized in this particular area and aware of potential triggering situations and how to address break-downs, should they occur. The instructor also does not physically touch without permission and knows how to place individuals in order to minimize feelings of vulnerabilities. Yoga therapy develops self-soothing and awareness techniques; assists participant in learning to self-regulate; restores balance within the body; allows relaxation to occur naturally; boosts immune function; and relieves stress and anxiety.

Expressive therapies include, but are not limited to: art, music, dance, drama, sand play, and expressive writing (Music and Expressive Therapies - One Page, 2018). Expressive therapy helps to unlock the emotional parts of the brain and assign words to emotions (Bessel Van Der Kolk, 2014). This type of therapy is extremely helpful for those who have difficulty verbalizing traumatic events. Expressive therapies promote; expression, imagination, active participation, and mind-body connection.

Music can help promote sleep, calm the body and mind, ease anxiety, encourage and energize the mind and body; and provides an opportunity to express and vent emotions. Experimenting with different kinds of art can push one to the edge of their comfort zone, promote self-exploration and trust, and create a safe place for expression with the use of group interaction (Music and Expressive Therapies - One Page, 2018).

Mindfulness, in its simplest form, is a technique used by groups and individuals to maintain a sense of being in the present time and place (Turow, 2017) (Watt, 2012). Some people carry "grounding" kits with them, and often include things that can be seen, touched, tasted, and smelled. Identifying and using items you can see, touch, taste, smell, and hear will often bring you back to center. For example, I often give presentations in my socks. While, they are adorable, they help me feel my feet on the ground and I can sense the texture of the socks. This helps me stay focused when drifting off. Mindfulness is an attempt to be in a non-judgmental and present-minded space.

Aroma therapy is a sensory-based intervention (Johnson, 2012). I would give caution with this one. It can be very helpful for individuals but if you are a practitioner, be aware that if you fill a room with a particular scent, you may create a trigger for the person or persons walking in to your office, classroom, or clinic. Some fragrances may be pleasant for you but very unsettling for others. Our sense of smell is the quickest way to memory.

Breathing techniques are very helpful to reset the body's internal systems (Lundberg, 2016). A common technique is to breathe in for 4 seconds through the nose, and then out for 8 seconds through the mouth. The act of breathing out settles down the heart and brain, bringing all systems back to homeostasis.

Animal assisted therapy is a great way to relieve stress, increase confidence, and allow an individual to build a relationship with something other than a person (Malchiodi, 2008). Therapy animals are often brought into courtrooms and other settings that help allow victims to stay focused and tell their story in linear way. Victims are often bombarded with fear and anxiety; therapy animals can help relieve those symptoms. Participating in animal assisted therapy is less threatening, provides comfort and support, promotes safety, increases attention and focus, reduces depression and anxiety, and increases motivation to participate in therapy.

Additional Therapeutic Methods include Emotionally Focused Therapy, Internal Family Systems Therapy, Somatic Therapy, Eye Movement Desensitization and Reprocessing Therapy, Dialectical Behavior Therapy, and Group Therapy.

Take-aways

- Helping victims is possible, if you can recognize the signs.
- Create a safe, non-judgmental, space for open communication.
- The first thing a victim needs to hear is "I believe you."
- There is hope! Several therapeutic interventions have been identified to help victims tap into the emotional parts of the brain and connect with language and logic. Through additional expressive, animal, aroma, yoga, and mindfulness therapies the narrative can begin to emerge.

Epilog

I want to thank you for taking the time to educate yourself on this horrific and devastating issue. The impact human trafficking has on the lives of all people, can no longer be ignored. You are part of a small group who have chosen to become aware of the issue, identify vulnerabilities, and take action! Whether you are a professional in the field, a family member, or a concerned community member; you ARE a first responder! You Rock!!

Terminology

Trafficking Terminology for Adults – Adopted from the Shared Hope International program "Chosen"

Domestic Minor Sex Trafficking (DMST) – DMST is the commercial sexual exploitation of American children within the United States. It is the recruitment, harboring, transporting, providing, or obtaining of a person for the purpose of a commercial sex act and the person is a United States citizen or lawful permanent resident under the age of 18.

The Game/The Life – the subculture of prostitution, complete with rules, a hierarchy of authority, and language. Referring to the act of pimping as 'the game' gives the illusion that it can be a fun and easy way to make money, when the reality is much different. Men, women, and children will say they've been "in the life" if they've been involved in prostitution.

Trafficker/Pimp – Anyone who receives money or something of value for the sexual exploitation of another person.

Facilitator – Any business or person allowing or assisting a trafficker to carry out his/her business. These facilitators (taxi drivers, hotel owners, backpage.com, etc.) benefit from the proceeds earned through the commercial sexual exploitation of children.

Buyer (or John) – An individual who pays for or trades something of value, for sexual acts. This can be anyone- a family member, teacher, coach, or member of the clergy. They can be male or female, young and old.

Survival Sex – A term referring to a situation that involves a minor providing sexual favors to an adult in exchange for basic needs such as shelter, food, or security. This often happens when minor homeless or runaways have little option to obtain basic physical/survival needs. Minors on the street are often approached by predators who exploit their needs. Instead of offering to help the youth find a safe place, the predator will take advantage of the minor for his/her own personal gain.

Daddy – The term a pimp will often require his victim to call him.

Family/Folks – The term used to describe the other people under the control of the same trafficker/pimp.

Bottom Bitch – One girl, among several controlled by a single pimp, appointed by him to supervise the others and report rule violations. They are often sent out to recruit and bring new victims to the pimp. Operating as his "right hand," the Bottom may help collect money, book hotel rooms, post ads, or inflict punishments on other girls. A pimp will strategically position his Bottom to take the fall if law enforcement uncovers the operation.

Sister Wife/Wifeys/Wife-in-Law – What women and girls under the control of the same pimp call each other.

Stable – A group of victims under the control of a single pimp.

Date – The exchange when prostitution takes place, or the activity of prostitution. A victim is said to be "with a date" or "dating."

Trick – An area of town known for prostitution activity. This can be the area around a group of strip clubs and pornography stores, or a particular stretch of street.

Circuit – A series of cities among which prostituted people are moved. One example would be the West Coast circuit of San Diego, Las Vegas, Portland, and the cities between. The term can also refer to a chain of states such as the "Minnesota pipeline" by which victims are moved through a series of locations from Minnesota to markets in New York.

Quota – A set amount of money that a trafficking victim must make each night before she can come "home." Quotas are often set between $300 and $2000. If the victim returns without meeting the quota, she is typically beaten and sent back out on the street to earn the rest. Quotas can vary based on geographic region, local events, etc.

Seasoning – The process of breaking down a victim's resistance to ensure compliance. It is a combination of psychological manipulation, gang rape, intimidation, sodomy, beatings, deprivation of food or sleep, isolation from friends or family and other sources of support, and threatening or holding hostage of a victim's children.

Turn Out – The act of the trafficker/pimp forcing his victim to perform sex acts with others; forced prostitution.

Reckless Eyeballing – A term which refers to the act of looking around instead of keeping your eyes on the ground. Eyeballing is against the Rules of the Game and could lead an untrained victim to "choose up" by mistake.

Choosing Up – The process by which a different pimp takes "ownership" of a victim. Victims are instructed to keep their eyes on the ground at all times. According to the Rules of the Game, when a victim makes eye contact with another pimp (accidentally or on purpose), she is choosing him to be her pimp. If the original pimp wants the victim back, he must pay a fee to the new pimp. When this occurs, he will force the victim to work harder to replace the money lost in transaction. (Reckless Eyeballing)

Trade Up/Trade Down – To move a victim like merchandise between pimps. Pimps are quick to get rid of victims who cause problems, or who don't make enough money. A pimp may trade one girl for another or trade with some exchange of money. The victims can be moved long distances rapidly – with a guard, overnight, and/or by air, if necessary.

Finesse Pimp/Romeo Pimp – One who prides himself on controlling others primarily through psychological manipulation. Although he may shower his victims with affection and gifts (especially during the recruitment phase), the threat of violence is always present.

Gorilla (or Guerilla) Pimp – A pimp who controls his victims almost entirely through physical violence and force.

Escort Service – An organization, operating chiefly via cell phone and the internet, which sends a victim to a buyer's location (an "outcall") or arranges for the buyer to come to a house or apartment (an "in-call"); this may be the workplace of a single woman or a small brothel. Some escort services are networked with others and can assemble large numbers of women for parties and conventions. Some serve those with fetishes, such as sex with children or sadomasochism.

Automatic – a term denoting the victim's "automatic" routine when her pimp is out of town, in jail, or otherwise not in direct contact with those he is prostituting. Victims are expected to comply with the rules and often do so out of fear of punishment or because they have been psychologically manipulated into a sense of loyalty or love. All money generated on "automatic" is turned over to the pimp.

Renegade – A person involved in prostitution without a pimp. Renegades are vulnerable to threats, harassment, and violence specifically intended to make them "choose" a pimp.

Lot Lizard – A derogatory term for a person who is prostituted at a truck stop.

Assessment Questions

Assessment Questions

Safety Check

- Are you in a safe place?
- Can you tell me where you are?
- If we get disconnected, how can I get a hold of you?
- Are you injured? Would you like me to call 911/an ambulance?

General Questions

- How old are you?
- Who are you living with?
- Do you have a permanent place to stay or do you go from place to place?
- Do you have access to transportation?

Fraud Questions

- How did you find out about your job/meet this person?
- What were you told about the job before you started?

- Did anything surprise you about this job/relationship?
- Did conditions of your job/relationship change over time?
- Were you forced to sign a contract you did not understand?

Coercion Questions

- Did you ever feel pressured to do something that you didn't want to do or felt uncomfortable doing?
- What were your expectations of what would happen if you left this person/situation or if you didn't do what this person told you to do?
- Did anyone ever take/keep your legal papers or identification for you, such as your passport, visa, driver's license, etc.?
- Did anyone ever threaten you or intimidate you?
- Did you ever feel that if you left the situation, something bad would happen?

Debt-Monetary Questions

- Do you have access to money you earn? Does anyone take you money or a portion of your money? Did anyone hold your money for "safe keeping"?
- Are you, or were you, required to make a certain amount of money per day/week? What will happen if you do not make this amount of money?

- Do you owe any money to anyone in the situation? If so, who do you owe money to and why?
- Do you feel it difficult to pay off your dept? Why?

Force Questions

- Does someone control, monitor or supervise your activity?
- Are you able to contact your friends and family? Is your access to communication limited or monitored?
- Are you allowed to leave the place you are living/working? Under what conditions?
- What do you think will happen if you leave the situation? Have you tried to leave? What happened?
- Did anyone ever force you to do something physically or sexually that you didn't feel comfortable doing?
- Were you ever physically abused? When? By who?
- Were you ever sexually abused? When? By who?
- Has anyone given you drugs, medication as way to control?

Sex Trafficking Assessment Questions

- Did anyone ever pressure you to engage in any sexual acts against you will?
- Did anyone ever force you to engage in sexual acts with friends or business associates for favors/money?

- Did anyone ever force you to engage in commercial sex through online websites, escort services, street prostitution, informal arrangements, brothels, fake massage businesses or strip clubs?
- Were you required to make a certain amount of money or meet a quota? What will happen if you do not make that amount of money or meet the quota?

References

References

9 Reasons Why Men Solicit. (2018). Retrieved from Shared Hope International: https://sharedhope.org/2018/04/9-reasons-why-men-solicit/

Bender, R. (2018). *Roadmap to redemption*. Lexington, KY.

Bessel A. Van Der Kolk, M. (2003). The neurobiology of childhood trauma and abuse. *Child and Adolescent Psychiatric Clinics*, 293-317.

Bessel Van Der Kolk, M. (2014). *The Body Keeps the Score: Brain, mind, and body in the healing of trauma*. New York: Penguin Books.

Bremner, J. D. M. (2006). Traumatic stress: effects on the brain. *Dialogues in Clinical Neuroscience*, 445-461.

Child Welfare and Human Trafficking; Issue Brief. (2015). Retrieved from Child Welfare : https://www.childwelfare.gov/pubPDFs/trafficking.pdf

Department of Health and Human Services. (2015). *Understanding the Effects of Maltreatment on Brain Development: Child Welfare Information Gateway*.

Roe-Sepowitz, D. C. J., Gallagher, C., Hogan, K., Ward, T., Bracey, K., & Bracy, N. (2017). *A six-year analysis of sex trafficking of minors*. Arizona State University Office of Sex Trafficking Intervention Research.

Fay, D. (2017). *Attachment-based yoga & meditation for trauma recovery*. New York: W.W. Norton & Company, Inc.

Felitti, D. V. (2018). ACE's Study. *SAFE Conference 2018*. Chicago.

Foster Care & Human Trafficking. (2017). Retrieved from CAS Research & Education: http://www.casre.org/our_children/fcht/

Gerassi, L. (2015). From exploitation to industry: Definitions, risks, and consequences of domestic sexual exploitation and sex work among women and girls. *J Hum Behav Soc Environ.*, 591-605. doi:10.1080/10911359.2014.991055

'Grooming' is a Gateway to Online Child Sex Trafficking. (2018). Retrieved from Freedom United.

Guirguis, M. (2018). Internet Sex Trafficking: Will the Monster Stop

Growing? *15th Annual International Human Trafficking and Social Justice Conference.* Toledo.

Handrahan, L. (2017). *Epidemic: America's Trade in Child Rape.* Chicago: Independent Publishers Group.

Harris, M. (1998). *Trauma Recovery and Empowerment.* New York: Simon & Schuster, Inc.

International, S. H. (2018). *Just Faith Summit.* St. Paul.

Jackman, T. (2017). House passes anti-online sex trafficking bill, allows targeting of websites like Backpage.com. *The Washington Post.*

Johnson, B. C. (2012). Aftercare for Survivors of Human Trafficking. *Journal of North American Association of Christians in Social Work,* 370-89.

Landers, M., McGrath, K., Johnson, M. H., Armstrong, M. I., & Dollard, N. (2017). Baseline characteristics of dependent youth who have been commercially sexually exploited: Findings from a specialized treatment program. *Journal of Child Sexual Abuse, 26*(6), 692-709.

Lundberg, M. E. (2016). *Identifying and healing childhood sexual abuse.* Columbia.

Macy, R. J., & Graham, L. M. (2012). Trauma, Violence, & Abuse: Identifying Domestic and International Sex-Trafficking Victims During Human Service Provision. *SAGE Publication.* Retrieved from http://tva.sagepub.com/content/13/2/59

Malchiodi, C. A. (2008). *Creative Interventions with Traumatized Children.* New York: The Guilford Press.

Monica Bucci, M., Silverio Marques DrPH, S., Oh, PhD, MSc, D., & Burke Harris, MD, MPH, N. (2016). Toxic stress in children and adolescents. *Advances in Pediatrics,* 403-428.

Music and Expressive Therapies - One Page. (2018). Retrieved from Trauma Recovery University.

National Center for Missing and Exploited Children. (2018). www.missingkids.org

Pinaki Mukherji, M. F. (2015). Recognizing human trafficking victims in the emergency department. *RELIAS.*

Project, P. (2016). *Human Trafficking Statistics.* Polaris Project. Retrieved from www.polarisproject.org

Reichert, J., & Sylwestrzak, A. (2013). *National survey of residential programs for victims of sex trafficking.* Illinois Criminal Justice Information Authority.

Roelofs, K. (2017). Freeze for action: neurobiological mechanisms in animal and human freezing. *Philos Trans R Soc Lond B Biol Sci.*

Roland C. Summit, M. (1983). The child sexual abuse accommodation syndrome. *Child Abuse and Neglect*, 177-193.

Sartory, G., Cwik, J., Knuppertz, H., Schurholt, B., Lebens, M., Seitz, R. J., & Schulze, R. (2013). In Search of the Trauma Memory: A Meta-Analysis of Functional Neuroimaging Studies of Symptom Provocation in Posttraumatic Stress Disorder (PTSD). *PLOS ONE.*

Seltzer Phd, L. F. (2015). Trauma and the freeze response: good, bad, or both? *Psychology Today.*

Services, U. D. (2013). *Guidance to States and Services on Addressing Human Trafficking of Children and Youth in the United States.* U.S. Department of Health and Human Services Administration for Children, Youth and Families (ACYF). Retrieved from http://www.state.gov/j/tip/rls/tiprpt/2013/

Social Judo. (2017). Retrieved from 26 apps used by online predators: https://www.socialjudo.com/2017/03/

State, U. D. (2016). *Trafficking in Persons Report June 2016.* Washington D.C.: U.S. Department of State. Retrieved from https://www.state.gov/documents/organization/258876.pdf

Syme, RDH, MS, S. L. (2017). Human trafficking: red flags for dental professionals. *Decisions in Dentistry.*

The Blue Knock Foundation. (2018).

The Victims and Traffickers. (2017). Retrieved from Polaris Project : https://polarisproject.org/victims-traffickers?gclid=Cj0KEQjww7zH-BRCToPSj_c_WjZIBEiQAj8il5NX-38NPyd-Vprh522e_AkQ9D83MzJs9bgV2uzwmdAaIaArLw8P8HAQ

Troopers, M. S. (January 21, 2018). Human Trafficking Conference. Durand, MI .

Turow, R. G. (2017). *Mindfulness skills for trauma and ptsd.* New York: W.W. Norton & Company, INC.

U.S. Department of State Office of Historian. (2016, March 5). Retrieved from U.S. Department of State: https://history.state.gov/milestones/1750-1775

Watt, T. (2012). *Mindfullness: A Practical Guide.* New York: MJF Books.

www.ingramcontent.com/pod-product-compliance
Lightning Source LLC
Chambersburg PA
CBHW050744030426
42336CB00012B/1647